The Fam Fondue Recipe Book

Fondue in A Melting Pot to Eat Together

By

Angel Burns

© 2019 Angel Burns, All Rights Reserved.

License Notices

This book or parts thereof might not be reproduced in any format for personal or commercial use without the written permission of the author. Possession and distribution of this book by any means without said permission is prohibited by law.

All content is for entertainment purposes and the author accepts no responsibility for any damages, commercially or personally, caused by following the content.

Table of Contents

Fancy Fondue Recipes 7

Chapter I - Non-Alcoholic Sweet 8

    Recipe 1: Mocha Fondue.................................... 9

    Recipe 2: Banana Bread Fondue 11

    Recipe 3: S'Mores Fondue 13

    Recipe 4: Cheesecake Fondue.. 15

    Recipe 5: Slow-Cooked Butterscotch Fondue 17

    Recipe 6: Chocolate Peanut Butter Fondue................... 19

    Recipe 7: Orange and Cardamom Chocolate Fondue ... 22

    Recipe 8: Cookie Dough Fondue 25

    Recipe 9: Lemon Fondue 27

    Recipe 10: Hot Fudge Fondue.. 29

Chapter II - Non-Alcoholic Savory................................... 31

    Recipe 11: Vegan Chickpea Fondue 32

Recipe 12: Artichoke Fondue 35

Recipe 13: Spicy Blue Cheese Fondue 37

Recipe 14: Asiago Cauliflower Fondue 39

Recipe 15: Pumpkin Fondue 42

Recipe 16: Chili Cheese Dog Fondue 45

Recipe 17: Pesto Fondue 47

Recipe 18: Croque Monsieur Fondue 50

Recipe 19: Goat Cheese Fondue with Fried Sage 52

Recipe 20: Dairy-Free Mushroom Fondue.................... 55

Chapter III - Boozy Sweet 58

Recipe 21: White Chocolate Peach Fondue 59

Recipe 22: Caramel and Dark Rum Fondue.................. 61

Recipe 23: Very Cherry Chocolate Fondue 64

Recipe 24: Chocolate Mint Fondue............................... 66

Recipe 25: Spiked Chocolate Hazelnut Fondue 68

Recipe 26: Creamy Raspberry Fondue.......................... 70

Recipe 27: Irish Cream Chocolate Fondue 73

Recipe 28: Dark Chocolate and Orange Liqueur Fondue 75

Recipe 29: Honey Champagne Fondue 77

Recipe 30: Grapefruit Fondue 80

Chapter IV - Boozy Savory 82

Recipe 31: Tarragon, Aniseed Liqueur, and Aged Gouda Cheese Fondue 83

Recipe 32: Beef and Red Wine Fondue 86

Recipe 33: Spicy Four Cheese Whiskey Fondue 89

Recipe 34: Cheese and Gin Fondue 92

Recipe 35: Irish Dubliner Fondue 94

Recipe 36: Cheese Fondue with Belgian Beer and Bourbon 97

Recipe 37: Chipotle and Tequila Cheesy Fondue 100

Recipe 38: Creamy Crab and Brandy Fondue 103

Recipe 39: Green Tomato Fondue 106

Recipe 40: Creamy Tomato and Vodka Fondue 109

About the Author 113

Author's Afterthoughts.. 115

Fancy Fondue Recipes

Chapter I - Non-Alcoholic Sweet

нннннннннннннннннннннннннннннннн

Recipe 1: Mocha Fondue

This mocha fondue is an excellent way to enjoy the two best things in life, coffee, and chocolate. Flavored with warm cinnamon, it's a great dessert to share with family and friends.

Yield: 6-8

Preparation Time: 15mins

Ingredient List:

- 3 cups milk chocolate chips
- ½ cup whipping cream
- 1 tablespoon instant coffee granules
- 2 tablespoons hot water
- 1 teaspoon vanilla essence
- ⅛ teaspoons ground cinnamon
- 1 (16 ounce) pound cake (cut into 10" cubes, to serve, optional)

HHHHHHHHHHHHHHHHHHHHHHHHHHHHHH

Instructions:

1. In a heavy pan, over low heat, melt the chocolate chips and cream while continually stirring.

2. In water, dissolve the coffee and add to the chocolate-cream mixture along with the vanilla essence and ground cinnamon. Mixing well to combine.

3. Serve warm with the cubes of cake.

Recipe 2: Banana Bread Fondue

This novel way to serve chocolate hazelnut fondue is a real showstopper.

Yield: 6-8

Preparation Time: 15mins

Ingredient List:

- 1 pound loaf of banana bread
- 2 cups chocolate hazelnut spread (warmed)
- 1 cup half-and-half
- 1 quart strawberries (to dip, optional)
- Shortbread cookies (to dip, optional)

HHHHHHHHHHHHHHHHHHHHHHHHHHHHHHH

Instructions:

1. Preheat the main oven to 425 degrees F.

2. Using a serrated kitchen knife, cut out the middle of the banana bread loaf leaving a 1" border.

3. Remove the middle of the loaf and cut into ½" pieces.

4. Transfer to a baking sheet and toast until crispy and golden, approximately 5-7 minutes.

5. In a bowl, whisk the warmed chocolate hazelnut spread with the half-and-half until silky smooth.

6. Pour the mixture into the carved out middle of the brad.

7. Serve with strawberries and cookies.

Recipe 3: S'Mores Fondue

Date night dessert or tempting treat, this spectacular S'mores fondue is simply the best.

Yield: 2

Preparation Time: 12mins

Ingredient List:

- ½ cup half-and-half
- Pinch of salt
- 12 ounces dark chocolate (chopped)
- 2 tablespoons sour cream
- Graham crackers (to serve, optional)
- Marshmallows (to serve, optional)

HHHHHHHHHHHHHHHHHHHHHHHHHHHHHH

Instructions:

1. In a medium pan, bring the half-and-half and salt to boil.

2. Remove from the heat and add the chocolate.

3. Set aside for 30 seconds before whisking in the sour cream until silky smooth.

4. Transfer to a fondue pot to keep warm and serve with graham crackers and marshmallows, for dipping.

Recipe 4: Cheesecake Fondue

Who doesn't love cheesecake? And this fondue version is simply the best. Serve with biscotti or cookies for that all-important crunch.

Yield: 8-12

Preparation Time: 15mins

Ingredient List:

- 1½ cups whipping cream
- 12 ounces cream cheese (cut into 1" cubes)
- ⅓ cup sugar
- 3 teaspoons freshly squeezed lemon juice
- 1½ teaspoons vanilla essence
- ¼ teaspoons cinnamon
- ⅛ teaspoons ground nutmeg
- Biscotti or cookies (to serve, optional)

HHHHHHHHHHHHHHHHHHHHHHHHHHHHHH

Instructions:

1. In a fondue pot, over moderate to low heat, simmer the cream.

2. Add the cream cheese, stirring until entirely melted and combined.

3. Stir in the sugar along with the fresh lemon juice, vanilla essence, cinnamon, and ground nutmeg.

4. Serve in the fondue pot and keep warm.

5. Serve with biscotti or cookies.

Recipe 5: Slow-Cooked Butterscotch Fondue

Whether you dip fruit, cake or cookies, this slow-cooked butterscotch fondue takes decidedly good.

Yield: 12-16

Preparation Time: 3hours

Ingredient List:

- 2 (14 ounce) cans sweetened condensed milk
- 2 cups packed brown sugar
- 1 cup butter (melted)
- ⅔ cup light corn syrup
- 1 teaspoon vanilla essence
- ¼ cup milk
- Cake cubes, cookies or fruit (to serve, optional)

HHHHHHHHHHHHHHHHHHHHHHHHHHHHH

Instructions:

1. Add the condensed milk, brown sugar, butter, corn syrup and vanilla essence to a 4-quart slow cooker and stir.

2. Cover and on low, cook for 3 hours.

3. Whisk in the milk until smooth and on low heat, keep warm, while occasionally stirring for up to 2 hours.

4. Serve with cake cubes, cookies or slices of fresh fruit.

Recipe 6: Chocolate Peanut Butter Fondue

This dairy-free fondue is party perfect; serve with crispy pretzels or fluffy marshmallows for crowd-pleasing dessert.

Yield: 10

Preparation Time: 15mins

Ingredient List:

- 1 (14 ounce) can coconut cream
- 10 ounces semi-sweet chocolate chips
- ¼ cup smooth peanut butter
- 3 tablespoons granulated sugar
- ⅛ teaspoons sea salt
- 1 tablespoon cocoa powder
- 2 teaspoons vanilla essence
- Peanut butter (to drizzle)
- Pretzels, marshmallows or angel cake (to serve, optional)

HHHHHHHHHHHHHHHHHHHHHHHHHHHHHH

Instructions:

1. In a pan, add the coconut cream along with the chocolate chips, peanut butter, sugar, and salt.

2. Over moderate to low heat, heat while whisking every 30 seconds, until the chocolate melts and the mixture is silky smooth.

3. Add the cocoa powder along with the vanilla essence until incorporated.

4. Transfer to a fondue pot.

5. Drizzle a swirl of peanut butter over the surface of the fondue and serve with pretzels, marshmallows or angel cake.

Recipe 7: Orange and Cardamom Chocolate Fondue

Orange and cardamom combine to make this a chocolate fondue with a difference.

Yield: 4

Preparation Time: 15mins

Ingredient List:

- ¾ cup whole milk
- 10 ounces bittersweet chocolate (finely chopped)
- ¾ teaspoons ground cardamom
- 2 tablespoons orange essence
- Pinch of salt

HHHHHHHHHHHHHHHHHHHHHHHHHHHHHH

Instructions:

5. Set up a double boiler.

6. Add the milk to a microwave-safe bowl and microwave on full power for 30 seconds, until steamy. Remove any skin that forms on the surface.

7. While the milk warms, remove the bowl from the top of the double boiler, and allow to cool.

8. Add the chopped chocolate to the bowl. Pour the hot milk over the top.

9. Set the bowl back over the double boiler, stirring until the chocolate is entirely melted.

10. Add the cardamom, along with the orange essence and salt.

11. Transfer to a fondue pot and serve with dippers of choice.

Recipe 8: Cookie Dough Fondue

Warm and melting cookie dough fondue, ready for dipping!

Yield: 4-6

Preparation Time: 15mins

Ingredient List:

- ¼ cup butter
- ¼ cup sugar
- ½ cup brown sugar
- 1 teaspoon vanilla essence
- ¾ cup flour
- 4 tablespoons heavy cream
- 3 tablespoons non-fat milk
- Mini chocolate chips (to garnish)

HHHHHHHHHHHHHHHHHHHHHHHHHHHHHH

Instructions:

1. Over low heat, in a pan, heat the butter.

2. Add the sugar and brown sugar, stirring until dissolved.

3. Add the vanilla essence along with the flour and cook, while stirring for 60 seconds.

4. Remove from the heat and whisk in the cream followed by the milk. Add additional milk if needed to achieve your preferred consistency.

5. Sprinkle the chocolate chips on the top and serve with your favorite dippers.

Recipe 9: Lemon Fondue

This citrus fondue is delicious served with gingerbread. The taste of sharp lemon is the perfect partner to warm and spicy ginger.

Yield: 10-12

Preparation Time: 10mins

Ingredient List:

- 1 cup sugar
- ½ cup cornstarch
- ½ teaspoons salt
- 4 cups water
- ½ cup butter (cubed)
- ½ cup freshly squeezed lemon juice
- 2 tablespoons lemon zest (grated)
- Gingerbread (to serve, optional)

HHHHHHHHHHHHHHHHHHHHHHHHHHHHHH

Instructions:

1. In a pan, combine the sugar with the cornstarch, and salt.

2. Pour in the water, stirring until silky smooth.

3. Bring to boil over moderate heat and cook while stirring for 1-2 minutes, until thickened.

4. Remove the pan from the heat and add the butter along with the freshly squeezed lemon juice and zest. Stir, until the butter is entirely melted.

5. Transfer the mixture to a fondue pot to keep warm.

6. Serve with gingerbread and enjoy.

Recipe 10: Hot Fudge Fondue

Say hello to the weekend with this hot and sweet fudgy fondue.

Yield: 4

Preparation Time: 10mins

Ingredient List:

- 1½ cups semi-sweet chocolate chips
- ½ cup half-and-half
- ¼ cup brown sugar
- ½ teaspoons instant coffee
- ½ teaspoons vanilla essence
- Pinch of salt

HHHHHHHHHHHHHHHHHHHHHHHHHHHHH

Instructions:

1. In a pan, combine the chocolate chips, half-and-half, brown sugar, coffee, vanilla essence, and salt. Over moderate heat, stir until silky smooth.

2. Serve with dippers of choice.

Chapter II – Non-Alcoholic Savory

HHHHHHHHHHHHHHHHHHHHHHHHHHHHHH

Recipe 11: Vegan Chickpea Fondue

Just because you are following a vegan lifestyle, doesn't mean you can't enjoy a delicious fondue! This spiced chickpea offering will please even your most meat-loving friends.

Yield: 4

Preparation Time: 15mins

Ingredient List:

- 2 (15 ounce) cans chickpeas (drained)
- 1 clove garlic (peeled)
- 2 cups vegetable stock
- ½ cup roasted red pepper
- 1 teaspoon white miso
- 1 teaspoon paprika
- 1 tablespoon tahini
- 2 tablespoons olive oil
- ½ teaspoons salt
- 2 tablespoons lemon juice
- 2 tablespoons nutritional yeast
- Crusty bread (cut into cubes, to serve)
- Veggie batons (to serve)

HHHHHHHHHHHHHHHHHHHHHHHHHHHHHHH

Instructions:

1. Add the chickpeas, garlic, stock, red pepper, miso, paprika, tahini, and olive oil to a food processor and blitz until smooth and combined.

2. Transfer the mixture to a saucepan over moderate heat and stir in the salt, lemon juice, and yeast.

3. Cook until hot through and serve with bread cubes and veggie batons.

Recipe 12: Artichoke Fondue

The fresh, citrusy flavor of artichoke compliments creamy, melting cheese fondue perfectly.

Yield: 12

Preparation Time: 30mins

Ingredient List:

- 2 cloves garlic (peeled, minced)
- 14½ ounces canned artichoke hearts (chopped)
- ¼ cup provolone cheese (shredded)
- 1½ cups mozzarella (shredded)
- ⅔ cup Parmesan (grated)
- ½ cup sour cream
- ½ cup mayonnaise
- Small handful fresh parsley (to garnish)

HHHHHHHHHHHHHHHHHHHHHHHHHHHHHHH

Instructions:

1. Preheat the main oven to 350 degrees F.

2. Combine all of the ingredients (the garlic, artichoke, provolone, mozzarella, Parmesan, sour cream, mayonnaise).

3. Place in the oven and bake for under half an hour until golden and bubbling.

Recipe 13: Spicy Blue Cheese Fondue

A pinch of cayenne pepper brings a tantalizing heat to this creamy blue cheese fondue.

Yield: 6

Preparation Time: 25mins

Ingredient List:

- 4 tablespoons unsalted butter
- 1 yellow onion (peeled, diced)
- ¼ cup all-purpose flour
- 2 cups whole milk
- 8 ounces blue cheese (crumbled)
- ¼ teaspoons cayenne pepper
- Kosher salt
- Potato chips and crackers (to serve)

HHHHHHHHHHHHHHHHHHHHHHHHHHHHHH

Instructions:

1. In a skillet over moderate heat, melt the butter and sauté the onion for 4-5 minutes until soft.

2. Stir in the flour and cook for 60 seconds.

3. Pour in the milk and whisk to combine, warm until thick.

4. Stir in the blue cheese, cayenne, and salt. When the cheese beings to melt, take off the heat and serve with potato chips and crackers.

Recipe 14: Asiago Cauliflower Fondue

If you love cauliflower cheese bake, then you'll adore these creamy, smoky fondue dish to share.

Yield: 6

Preparation Time: 20mins

Ingredient List:

- 1½ pounds cauliflower florets
- 1 cup heavy cream
- 2 teaspoons lemon juice
- 2 tablespoons unsalted butter (cut into cubes, softened)
- ½ teaspoons smoked paprika
- ¾ teaspoons salt
- ½ cup Asiago cheese (grated)

HHHHHHHHHHHHHHHHHHHHHHHHHHHHHH

Instructions:

1. Fit a saucepan with a steamer basket and fill with 2" of water. Bring to a boil and add the cauliflower, cover with a lid and cook for several minutes until tender. Allow to cool a little.

2. Add half of the cooled cauliflower to a food processor along with half of the cream. Pulse until combined.

3. Add the remaining cauliflower and cream to the processor and pulse again until combined.

4. Scrape down the bowl of the processor and add the lemon juice, butter, paprika, and salt. Blitz until smooth.

5. Add the grated cheese and pulse until combined.

6. Transfer the mixture to a saucepan over moderately low heat and cook for 5-6 minutes until hot through.

7. Spoon into a fondue pot and serve.

Recipe 15: Pumpkin Fondue

Pumpkin is a superb alternative to cheese. It has fewer calories but is packed full of flavor.

Yield: 10-12

Preparation Time: 15mins

Ingredient List:

Spice Mix:

- 1 tablespoon cinnamon
- ½ teaspoons allspice
- ¼ teaspoons nutmeg
- ¼ teaspoons cloves
- ⅛ teaspoons ground ginger

Fondue:

- 1 clove garlic (peeled, smashed)
- 1¾ cup crisp non-alcoholic apple cider
- ¾ cup fresh pumpkin puree
- ¼ teaspoons dry mustard powder
- ¼ teaspoons cayenne pepper
- ¼ teaspoons mixed spices (see recipe)
- ½ teaspoons sea salt
- 2 tablespoons unbleached all-purpose flour
- ½ cup Cheddar cheese (grated)
- ¼ cup Gruyère cheese (grated)
- 3 ounces Brie cheese (rind removed)
- 1 teaspoon freshly squeezed lemon juice
- Apple slices (to serve)

Instructions:

1. To make the spice mix: In a bowl, combine the cinnamon with the allspice, nutmeg, cloves, and ground ginger. Store in a resealable, air-tight container, until needed. This recipe will yield 2 tablespoons

2. To prepare the fondue. In a pan combine the garlic with the non-alcoholic cider, pumpkin, mustard powder, cayenne pepper, homemade mixed spices, and salt, occasionally whisk until incorporated.

3. Continue to cook over moderate heat until the mixture just comes to boil.

4. Turn the heat down to moderate low.

5. While the mixture heats, combine the flour with the Cheddar, Gruyere and Brie cheeses. The cheeses need to be added in 3 batches, whisking well in between additions, until melted.

6. Whisk in the lemon juice, and transfer the mixture to a fondue pot.

7. Serve with slices of apples.

Recipe 16: Chili Cheese Dog Fondue

Ditch the fancy fondue for a change and get dipping in this comforting, home-style chilli cheese dog offering. Even the kids will love it!

Yield: 8

Preparation Time: 15mins

Ingredient List:

- 1 pound Cheddar cheese (cubed)
- 30 ounces canned chili without free beans
- Pigs in blankets (for dipping)

HHHHHHHHHHHHHHHHHHHHHHHHHHHHHH

Instructions:

1. In a saucepan over moderate heat, combine the cheese and chili. Cook, while stirring, until the cheese melts.

2. Transfer to a serving pot alongside pigs in blankets dippers.

Recipe 17: Pesto Fondue

This fancy fondue is flavored with green pesto and three different types of cheese.

Yield: 4

Preparation Time: 20mins

Ingredient List:

- 8 ounces mozzarella cheese (shredded)
- 3 ounces Muenster cheese (shredded)
- 3 ounces Fontina cheese (shredded)
- 1½ tablespoons cornstarch
- ½ tablespoons olive oil
- 1 clove garlic (peeled, minced)
- 1 cup white wine
- ¼ cup green pesto
- Veggie batons (to dip, optional)

HHHHHHHHHHHHHHHHHHHHHHHHHHHHHH

Instructions:

1. In a bowl, combine the mozzarella with the Muenster and Fontina cheeses with the cornstarch.

2. In a fondue pot, over moderate heat, heat the oil. Add the garlic, cooking until fragrant.

3. Pour in the wine, and bring to simmer.

4. One handful at a time, add the cheese, whisking between additions to melt.

5. When the cheeses are entirely melted, fold in the pesto.

6. Place the fondue pot over the burner, set on moderate to low.

7. Serve with veggie dippers of choice.

Recipe 18: Croque Monsieur Fondue

All the flavor of the classic French sandwich in a melting pot of deliciousness.

Yield: 4

Preparation Time: 15mins

Ingredient List:

- 2 tablespoons butter
- 1 tablespoon flour
- ½ cup dry white wine
- 8 ounces gruyere cheese (grated)
- Salt and black pepper
- 20 cornichons
- 5 rashers cooked bacon (sliced into pieces)
- 1 small French baguette (cut into cubes)

HHHHHHHHHHHHHHHHHHHHHHHHHHHHHHH

Instructions:

1. In a saucepan over moderate heat, melt the butter. Whisk in the flour for 60 seconds, followed by the wine. When the mixture is simmering, add the grated cheese.

2. When the cheese has melted, season to taste and take off the heat. Transfer to a serving bowl.

3. Spear the cornichons, cooked bacon, and pieces of baguette on skewers and serve along the cheese fondue.

Recipe 19: Goat Cheese Fondue with Fried Sage

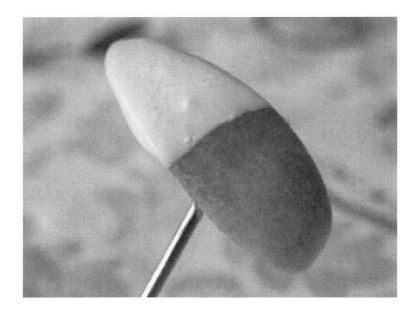

Make and share this goat cheese fondue with earthly tasting fried sage. Its pine-like flavor is the perfect complement to salt goat cheese.

Yield: 4-6

Preparation Time: 30mins

Ingredient List:

- ¾ cup dry white wine
- 2 garlic cloves (peeled, finely minced)
- ¾ cup heavy cream
- 16 ounces goat cheese
- Pinch of salt
- Dash of pepper
- Pinch of nutmeg
- 1 teaspoon olive oil
- 3 tablespoons unsalted butter
- 10-15 sage leaves
- Cubes of bread, veggies or fruit (to serve, optional)

HHHHHHHHHHHHHHHHHHHHHHHHHHHHHHH

Instructions:

1. Add the wine and garlic to a pan and bring to simmer.

2. Add the heavy cream, stir to combine and add the goat cheese. Reduce the heat to low and stir for several minutes until the cheese is entirely melted.

3. Season with a pinch of salt, a dash of pepper and a pinch of nutmeg. Taste and season more if necessary.

4. While the goat cheese melts, heat a pan over moderate heat and add the olive oil along with the butter. When the mixture, melts and bubbles, add the sage leaves, frying for 1-2 minutes, while not allowing the butter to burn. Remove and allow to drain on kitchen paper towel.

5. When you are ready to serve, crumble a few sage leaves into the fondue, stirring thoroughly to combine. Garnish the fondue with the remaining leaves and serve with bread, veggies or fresh fruit.

Recipe 20: Dairy-Free Mushroom Fondue

The yeast in this recipe adds a gentle cheese-like flavor to an already flavorsome fondue.

Yield: 6-8

Preparation Time: 15mins

Ingredient List:

- 5 tablespoons dairy-free margarine (divided)
- 3 garlic cloves (peeled, minced)
- ½ onion (peeled, minced)
- 2 cups mushrooms (sliced)
- 2 cups soy milk
- ½ teaspoons miso
- 1 bouillon cube
- 1 teaspoon onion powder
- ¼ cup flour
- ½ teaspoons celery salt
- 1 tablespoon soy sauce
- 3 tablespoons nutritional yeast
- Baby new potatoes (halved, to serve, optional)
- Tofu (to serve, optional)

HHHHHHHHHHHHHHHHHHHHHHHHHHHHH

Instructions:

1. In a skillet or frying pan, melt 3 tablespoons of margarine, and sauté the garlic, onions, and mushrooms until softened, set to one side.

2. In a second pan, over moderate to low heat, combine the soy milk with the miso, bouillon cube. Stir until incorporated and the bouillon cube is entirely dissolved.

3. Add the onion powder along with the flour, celery salt, soy sauce, and nutritional yeast, and bring to a gentle simmer, stirring to combine until thickened. If the mixture is not sufficiently thickened, add additional flour, and increase the heat slightly. Set aside to cool.

4. Add the sautéed mushrooms, garlic and onion mixture to the flour-yeast mixture and in a food blender, process until silky smooth.

5. Reheat the fondue while occasionally stirring, and allow to slightly cool before transferring to the fondue pot.

6. Serve with baby potatoes or tofu.

Chapter III – Boozy Sweet

HHHHHHHHHHHHHHHHHHHHHHHHHHHHH

Recipe 21: White Chocolate Peach Fondue

Peaches and cream go together like Mickey and Minnie and this sweet and chocolatey fondue to serve with crunchy meringue cookies is peach perfect.

Yield: 4

Preparation Time: 15mins

Ingredient List:

- ¾ cup heavy cream
- 12 ounces white morsels
- 1 (14½ ounce) can peaches (drained, pureed)
- ¼ cup white chocolate liqueur
- 1 package meringue cookies

HHHHHHHHHHHHHHHHHHHHHHHHHHHHHH

Instructions:

1. In a pan, heat the cream over moderate heat until bubbles form around the edges. Remove from the heat.

2. Add the white morsels, whisking until entirely melted and silky smooth.

3. Stir in the peach puree followed by the liqueur.

4. Transfer the mixture to a fondue pot and keep warm.

5. Serve with the meringue cookies.

Recipe 22: Caramel and Dark Rum Fondue

A winning dessert fondue for all those non-chocolate lovers out there.

Yield: 4-6

Preparation Time: 30mins

Ingredient List:

- 1 cup firmly packed brown sugar
- 1 cup white sugar
- ½ cup light corn syrup
- ¼ cup water
- 1½ cups heavy whipping cream
- ½ cup unsalted butter (room temperature)
- 2 tablespoons dark rum
- 2 teaspoons pure vanilla essence
- Pinch kosher salt

HHHHHHHHHHHHHHHHHHHHHHHHHHHHHH

Instructions:

1. In a deep-sided pan, combine the brown sugar with the white sugar, corn syrup, and water over moderate heat. Bring to boil while frequently stirring.

2. Cook until the mixture bubbles and becomes deep amber in color, approximately 10 minutes. Remove the pan from the heat.

3. Add the whipping cream and butter. The mixture should violently bubble.

4. Vigorously stir to combine the cream and butter into the sugar mixture.

5. Return to low heat and add the dark rum followed by the vanilla essence and a pinch of salt.

6. Stir the mixture until creamy smooth, for approximately 2 minutes.

7. Transfer the mixture to a fondue pot on low heat.

8. Serve with dippers of choice.

Recipe 23: Very Cherry Chocolate Fondue

Cherry brandy gives this chocolate fondue a boozy kick.

Yield: 4-6

Preparation Time: 20mins

Ingredient List:

- 2 cups milk chocolate chips
- 3 tablespoons heavy cream
- 2 tablespoons cherry brandy
- 1 tablespoon strong brewed coffee
- ⅛ teaspoons ground cinnamon
- Pineapple, banana, and mini mallows (to serve)

HHHHHHHHHHHHHHHHHHHHHHHHHHHHHH

Instructions:

1. In a fondue pot, over low heat, combine the chocolate chips with the heavy cream, cherry brandy, brewed coffee, and ground cinnamon.

2. Heat the mixture, while occasionally stirring, until entirely melted and smooth.

3. Serve with pieces of pineapple, bananas, or mini mallows.

Recipe 24: Chocolate Mint Fondue

Rich, dark and decadent. In fact, everything you are looking for in a dinner-party dessert.

Yield: 4-6

Preparation Time: 15mins

Ingredient List:

- 12 ounces dark chocolate (finely chopped)
- ½ cup heavy cream
- 3 tablespoons mint chocolate liqueur or crème de menthe

HHHHHHHHHHHHHHHHHHHHHHHHHHHHHHH

Instructions:

1. In a double boiler combine the chocolate and heavy cream, heating and continue stirring until entirely melted.

2. Transfer to a warm fondue pot.

3. Add the mint chocolate liqueur, stir to incorporate.

4. Over low heat, keep the fondue warm and serve with fresh fruit, cookies or marshmallows.

Recipe 25: Spiked Chocolate Hazelnut Fondue

Why go out when you can make chocolate fondue at home? Your friends and family will love this sweet dessert.

Yield: 4-6

Preparation Time: 15mins

Ingredient List:

- 2 cups heavy cream
- 14 ounces premium milk chocolate chips
- ½ cup chocolate hazelnut vodka
- Fresh berries, biscotti, brownie bites (to serve)

HHHHHHHHHHHHHHHHHHHHHHHHHHHHHH

Instructions:

1. In a pan, bring the cream to simmer.

2. Once the cream is simmering, add the chocolate chips along with the flavored vodka, stirring continually until entirely combined. Add additional chocolate chips if needed to thicken.

3. Serve the fondue warm with fresh berries, biscotti or brownie bites.

Recipe 26: Creamy Raspberry Fondue

The sweetness of raspberries combines with whipped cream cheese for a truly decadent delicious dessert.

Yield: 4-6

Preparation Time: 20mins

Ingredient List:

- 2 (10 ounce) packs frozen raspberries (thawed)
- ¼ cup cornstarch
- ½ cup cold water
- 1 (4 ounce) tub whipped cream cheese (room temperature)
- 2 tablespoons granulated sugar
- ¼ cup brandy
- Fresh fruit and cake cubes (to serve)

HHHHHHHHHHHHHHHHHHHHHHHHHHHHHH

Instructions:

1. In a pan, using the back of a wooden spoon, slightly crush the raspberries.

2. In a bowl, blend the cornstarch with the water and add the raspberries.

3. Cook, while stirring until thickened and bubbly.

4. Sieve the mixture with a fine mesh sieve, and discard the seeds.

5. Transfer the mixture to a fondue pot and set over a fondue burner.

6. Add the cream cheese, stirring well until entirely melted.

7. Stir in the sugar, while a little at a time, adding the brandy.

8. Serve with fresh fruit or cubes of cake, for dipping.

Recipe 27: Irish Cream Chocolate Fondue

A good slug of Irish Cream liqueur gives this chocolate fondue a decadent boozy flavor.

Yield: 6

Preparation Time: 25mins

Ingredient List:

- 9 ounces semi-sweet baking chocolate (coarsely chopped)
- ¼ cup heavy cream
- ¼ cup Irish cream liqueur
- Banana, marshmallows, and cake dippers (to serve)

HHHHHHHHHHHHHHHHHHHHHHHHHHHHHH

Instructions:

1. Add the chocolate, heavy cream and Irish cream liqueur to a fondue pot and over low heat, cook, while constantly stirring until the chocolate is smooth and entirely melted.

2. Serve with bananas, marshmallows, or cake dippers.

Recipe 28: Dark Chocolate and Orange Liqueur Fondue

Chocolate and orange are two flavors that come together in perfect harmony and this fondue to serve with fresh fruit of gooey marshmallows is simply scrumptious.

Yield: 4

Preparation Time: 15mins

Ingredient List:

- ⅔ cup heavy whipping cream
- 2 (8 ounce) bars dark baking chocolate (finely chopped)
- 1 teaspoon orange liqueur
- 1 teaspoon orange peel (grated)
- Fruit, pretzels, and marshmallows (to serve)

HHHHHHHHHHHHHHHHHHHHHHHHHHHHHH

Instructions:

1. Over moderate to high heat, in a small pan, heat the cream, and bring to boil. Remove the pan from the heat.

2. Add the chopped chocolate, stirring until smooth. Add the orange liqueur along with the orange peel, mixing well to combine.

3. Transfer the mixture to a fondue pot, and place over low heat.

4. Serve with fruit, pretzels or marshmallows.

Recipe 29: Honey Champagne Fondue

Cheese and honey are the perfect pairing but add Champagne to the mix, and you have an elegant fondue to share.

Yield: 6-8

Preparation Time: 30mins

Ingredient List:

- ¼ cup shallots (finely chopped)
- 1 tablespoon butter
- 1 clove garlic (peeled, minced)
- 1¼ cups Champagne
- 4 teaspoons cornstarch
- 1 teaspoon ground mustard
- ¼ teaspoons white pepper
- ⅓ cup honey
- 4 cups Swiss cheese (shredded)
- 2 tablespoons freshly squeezed lemon juice
- Pinch ground nutmeg

HHHHHHHHHHHHHHHHHHHHHHHHHHHHHH

Instructions:

1. In a large pan, sauté the shallot in the butter until fork tender.

2. Add the garlic and sauté for an additional 60 seconds.

3. In a bowl, combine the Champagne with the cornstarch, ground mustard, and white pepper until silky smooth. Gradually stir the mixture into the pan and bring to boil, and continue to cook, while stirring for a couple of minutes, until thickened.

4. Stir in the honey and heat through. Remove from the heat.

5. In a bowl, combine the cheese with the fresh lemon juice, and a little at a time stir it into the Champagne mixture until entirely melted.

6. Garnish the fondue with nutmeg and serve with your favorite dipper.

Recipe 30: Grapefruit Fondue

The bitterness of the grapefruit when paired with a herbal liqueur and served with sweet melon delivers an exciting and sophisticated fondue.

Yield: 6

Preparation Time: 15mins

Ingredient List:

- 3 tablespoons sugar
- 3 tablespoons Italian herbal liqueur
- 1 tablespoon cornstarch
- Freshly squeezed juice of 2 large grapefruit
- 1 tablespoon grapefruit peel (finely grated)
- 3 tablespoons heavy cream
- Sprig of mint (to garnish)
- 1 honeydew melon (peeled, seeded, scooped into balls)

HHHHHHHHHHHHHHHHHHHHHHHHHHHHHH

Instructions:

1. Combine the sugar, Italian herbal liqueur and cornstarch in a pan and stir until smooth.

2. Stir in the fresh grapefruit juice along with the peel and bring to boil, constantly stirring, and simmer for 60 seconds.

3. Remove the pan from the heat, stir in the heavy cream and transfer to the fondue pot.

4. Garnish with a sprig of mint and serve warm with the melon balls.

Chapter IV – Boozy Savory

HHHHHHHHHHHHHHHHHHHHHHHHHHHHHH

Recipe 31: Tarragon, Aniseed Liqueur, and Aged Gouda Cheese Fondue

A true taste of old Amsterdam, this super tasty fondue features aged Gouda which packs a powerful punch combined with aniseed liqueur.

Yield: 6

Preparation Time: 45mins

Ingredient List:

- 10 ounces white wine
- 7 ounces aged Gouda cheese (grated)
- 7 ounces Gruyere cheese (grated)
- 1 garlic clove (peeled)
- 1 shot of aniseed liqueur
- 1 tablespoon cornflour
- Dash of white pepper
- Pinch of nutmeg
- Tarragon leaves (chopped, to garnish)
- Crusty French baguette (sliced, to serve, optional)

HHHHHHHHHHHHHHHHHHHHHHHHHHHHHH

Instructions:

1. Add the wine to a pan and bring to simmer.

2. Gradually, add the grated Gouda and Gruyere cheeses, allowing them to entirely melt over low heat.

3. Grate the garlic above the pan and stir to combine.

4. In a small bowl, combine the aniseed liqueur with the cornflour, to form a smooth paste. Add the paste to the pan. Season with white pepper and nutmeg, allowing the mixture to simmer for 2-3 minutes until thickened.

5. Transfer the mixture to a fondue pan and garnish with tarragon.

6. Serve with slices of crusty bread.

Recipe 32: Beef and Red Wine Fondue

Transform a traditional beef broth fondue with a dry, tart red wine.

Yield: 4

Preparation Time: 25mins

Ingredient List:

- 1 pound boneless beef sirloin steak (sliced thinly across the grain)
- ¾ cup button mushrooms
- ¾ cup red onion wedges
- ¾ cup broccoli florets
- 1 (30 ounce) carton 30% reduced-salt beef broth
- ¾ cup Syrah red wine
- ⅓ cup onion (peeled, minced)
- 1 teaspoon fresh thyme leaves (finely chopped)
- ⅛ teaspoons ground black pepper
- 1 bay leaf
- Crusty bread

HHHHHHHHHHHHHHHHHHHHHHHHHHHHHHH

Instructions:

1. Arrange the beef together with the button mushrooms, red onion, and broccoli on a serving platter. Set to one side.

2. In a pan, bring the broth, red wine, onion, thyme leaves, black pepper, and bay leaf to a pan and simmer for 10 minutes.

3. Pour the mixture into a fondue pot and simmer while the meat and veggies are cooked through.

4. Serve with crusty bread.

Recipe 33: Spicy Four Cheese Whiskey Fondue

Say yes please to cheese, with this spicy oeey gooey cheesy, fondue-infused with whiskey.

Yield: 4-6

Preparation Time: 25mins

Ingredient List:

- 4 ounces aged white Cheddar (grated)
- 4 ounces Gruyere (grated)
- 4 ounces Fontina cheese (grated)
- 4 ounces Monterey Jack cheese (grated)
- 2 tablespoons cornstarch
- 2 cloves garlic (peeled, halved)
- 1 cup dry white wine
- 4 tablespoons whiskey
- Salt and pepper
- Chili powder
- 5 slices Italian white bread (cut into cubes)

HHHHHHHHHHHHHHHHHHHHHHHHHHHHHH

Instructions:

1. Add the grated cheeses to a bowl. Add the cornstarch and using clean hands, combine.

2. Rub the cut side of the garlic onto the inside of a large pan, then discard.

3. Over moderate heat, bring the white wine to a simmer.

4. Add the cheeses in 4 batches, whisking after each addition until the cheese entirely melts.

5. A little at a time, add the whiskey, stirring until it comes to boil.

6. When the mixture begins to boil, remove it from the heat. Season to taste with salt and pepper and add a pinch of chili powder, to taste.

7. Serve with cubes of bread.

Recipe 34: Cheese and Gin Fondue

Sometimes the evenings are better spent indoors with your favorite person, plus of course a warm pot of boozy fondue.

Yield: 2

Preparation Time: 20mins

Ingredient List:

- 1¾ cups dry white wine
- 1 pound Gruyere cheese (grated)
- ¼ cup gin
- 3 teaspoons cornstarch
- ½ garlic clove (peeled)
- Ground nutmeg
- Ground black pepper
- Veggie batons (to serve)

HHHHHHHHHHHHHHHHHHHHHHHHHHHHHH

Instructions:

1. Add the wine to a fondue pot and heat.

2. Gradually stir in the cheese, until entirely melted.

3. In a bowl, combine the gin with the cornstarch, mixing until dissolved and add to the fondue pot.

4. Add the garlic clove and stir. Bring to boil and season with the nutmeg and black pepper.

5. Add additional cornstarch- gin to thicken, or wine to thin.

6. Serve with veggie batons.

Recipe 35: Irish Dubliner Fondue

This fondue is more of a main than an appetizer. It ticks all the taste boxes!

Yield: 4

Preparation Time: 15mins

Ingredient List:

- 1¼ cups pale Irish beer
- 1 clove garlic (peeled, cracked)
- 8 ounces Dubliner or mature Cheddar cheese (shredded)
- 1 tablespoon flour
- 2 teaspoons ground mustard
- Black pepper
- Boiled baby potatoes (to serve)

HHHHHHHHHHHHHHHHHHHHHHHHHHHHHH

Instructions:

1. Add a small pan over moderate heat.

2. Pour the beer into the pan along with the cracked garlic.

3. In a bowl, combine the cheese with the flour along with the mustard.

4. Gradually, add the cheese-flour mixture to the beer, whisking until silky smooth for 5-10 minutes, until it thickens.

5. Once the mixture is thickened and smoothed transfer it to fondue pot.

6. Serve with baby boiled potatoes.

Recipe 36: Cheese Fondue with Belgian Beer and Bourbon

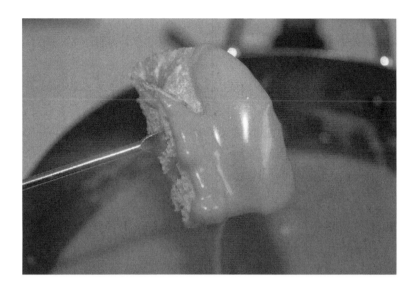

Definitely one for the grown-ups! Belgian beer and bourbon fondue with Gruyere and Babybel cheeses make a great game night meal to share.

Yield: 4

Preparation Time: 20mins

Ingredient List:

- 2 cloves garlic (halved lengthwise)
- ½ cup Belgian beer
- 2 cups dry white wine
- 3 tablespoons cornstarch
- 1 pound Babybel cheese (grated)
- 1 pound Gruyere cheese (grated)
- 2 tablespoons bourbon
- ¼ teaspoons baking soda
- 1 tablespoon freshly squeezed lemon juice
- Kosher salt
- Cold meats (to serve, optional)
- Pickles (to serve, optional)
- 4 cups (1" thick) slices, day-old, country-style bread (to serve, optional)

HHHHHHHHHHHHHHHHHHHHHHHHHHHHHH

Instructions:

1. Rub the cut sides of the garlic cloves inside a large pan. Finely grate the garlic into the pan.

2. Pour in the beer along with 1½ cups of white wine, bring to boil over moderate heat.

3. In a small bowl, whisk in the cornstarch along with the remaining wine. When lump-free whisk the mixture into the garlic-wine mixture.

4. Bring to boil while constantly whisking before reducing the heat to a very low simmer.

5. A little at a time add the cheeses, stirring in-between additions until entirely combined.

6. In a bowl, whisk the bourbon with the baking soda to incorporate. Whisk into the fondue along with the fresh lemon juice. Season to taste, with salt.

7. Transfer the mixture to a fondue pot and serve with a selection of cold meats, pickles, and bread.

Recipe 37: Chipotle and Tequila Cheesy Fondue

Travel south for a Mexican-inspired fondue with tequila, and spicy chipotle.

Yield: 4

Preparation Time: 25mins

Ingredient List:

- 1½ tablespoons cornstarch
- ¼ cup reposado tequila
- 1 cup dry white wine
- 8 ounces Monterey Jack cheese (grated)
- 12 ounces aged Fontina cheese (grated)
- 2-3 teaspoons chipotle in spicy adobo sauce (pureed)
- ¼ teaspoons sea salt
- 1 sourdough baguette (cut into ½" cubes)

HHHHHHHHHHHHHHHHHHHHHHHHHHHHHH

Instructions:

1. Add the cornstarch along with the tequila to a bowl and set to one side.

2. Pour the wine into a pan and over moderate to high heat, heat to a simmer.

3. A little at a time, add the grated Monterey Jack cheese along with the aged Fontina, continually whisking until entirely melted and lump-free.

4. Reduce the heat to moderate and add the cornstarch-tequila mixture along with the chipotle and salt. Continue whisking for between 1-2 minutes, until the mixture slightly thickens.

5. Transfer the mixture to a fondue pot over a flame to keep it warm.

6. Serve with the cubes of sourdough bread.

Recipe 38: Creamy Crab and Brandy Fondue

You are sure to become the hostess with the mostest when you serve this dinner-party worthy fondue.

Yield: 4-6

Preparation Time: 35mins

Ingredient List:

- 1 tablespoon unsalted butter
- 1 tablespoon olive oil
- ¼ cup shallots (minced)
- 2 cloves garlic, finely minced
- ½ teaspoons cayenne pepper
- 1 teaspoon dried Italian seasoning
- 1 cup dry white wine
- ¼ cup brandy
- 1 pound cream cheese
- 3 cups whipping cream
- 1 pound lump crab meat
- Salt and ground black pepper
- Garlic bread (to serve, optional)

HHHHHHHHHHHHHHHHHHHHHHHHHHHHHH

Instructions:

1. Over low heat, in a pot, heat the butter and oil.

2. Add the shallots and cook for 5 minutes, occasionally stirring.

3. Next, add the garlic followed by the cayenne pepper and Italian seasoning and cook for 1 minute, stirring as necessary.

4. Pour in the white wine along with the brandy and over high heat, bring to boil before reducing to a simmer over moderate heat and cooking, while occasionally stirring for 10 minutes.

5. While the mixture simmers, in a bowl, combine the cream cheese with the whipping cream and mix to combine.

6. Add the cream cheese-cream mixture to the pot and mix until silky smooth.

7. Finally, add the crab meat and season. Stir well and transfer to a fondue pot.

8. Serve with garlic bread and enjoy.

Recipe 39: Green Tomato Fondue

This tomato fondue with feta cheese and ouzo served with warm pita will transport you straight to the Greek islands.

Yield: 6

Preparation Time: 45mins

Ingredient List:

- 3 green tomatoes (halved lengthwise)
- Salt and pepper
- ½ cup ouzo
- ½ cup dry white wine
- ½ cup of extra virgin Greek olive oil
- 3 cups goats' milk feta (crumbled)
- ½ cup water
- ½ cup mixed herbs (chopped, of choice)
- 3 warm pita breads (halved, to serve, optional)

HHHHHHHHHHHHHHHHHHHHHHHHHHHHHHH

Instructions:

1. Preheat the main oven to 350 degrees F.

2. Add the green tomatoes to a baking dish and season all over.

3. Pour in the ouzo, followed by the white wine and olive oil.

4. Flip the tomatoes onto their cut side and roast in the preheated oven for between 20-25 minutes, until fork tender.

5. Allow the green tomatoes to cool for 8-10 minutes, in order for their juices to release. Set the juices aside.

6. Add the crumbled feta to a food processor; add the tomato juices along with the water. Process until creamy smooth; this will take a couple of minutes.

7. Pour the feta mixture into the baking dish containing the halves of tomatoes.

8. Bake in the oven until bubbly and soft, for 10 minutes.

9. Garnish with mixed herbs and serve with warm pita.

Recipe 40: Creamy Tomato and Vodka Fondue

Forget the vodka pasta, instead opt for this fancy fondue. Serve with large cooked shrimp for the wow factor.

Yield: 8-12

Preparation Time: 1hour 20mins

Ingredient List:

- 2 tablespoons virgin olive oil
- 1 medium onion (peeled, chopped)
- 1 teaspoon salt
- 2 cloves garlic (peeled, minced)
- ½ teaspoons crushed hot red pepper
- 2 (28 ounce) cans crushed tomatoes
- ½ cup vodka
- ½ cup heavy cream
- ½ cup Parmesan cheese (freshly grated)
- 1½ tablespoons slivered fresh basil

HHHHHHHHHHHHHHHHHHHHHHHHHHHHHH

Instructions:

1. Over moderate heat, in a large stainless steel or ceramic skillet heat the oil.

2. Add the onion and season. Cook, while occasionally stirring for 3-5 minutes, until the onions are not browned, but softened.

3. Stir in the minced garlic along with the hot pepper flakes and cook for an additional 30 seconds.

4. Add the tomatoes and pour in the vodka, stirring to combine.

5. Turn the heat down to moderate to low and uncovered, simmer for 60 minutes, while occasionally stirring, until thickened.

6. Add the heavy cream and stir, cooking for an additional 5 minutes. Remove from the heat and fold in the grated Parmesan.

7. Using a blender, puree the sauce in the pot until silky smooth. You may need to reheat.

8. Transfer the sauce to a fondue pot and garnish with basil. The fondue should be kept warm and not hot.

9. Serve with garlic bread, large cooked shrimp, cubes of chicken or cubes of polenta.

About the Author

Angel Burns learned to cook when she worked in the local seafood restaurant near her home in Hyannis Port in Massachusetts as a teenager. The head chef took Angel under his wing and taught the young woman the tricks of the trade for cooking seafood. The skills she had learned at a young age helped her get accepted into Boston University's Culinary Program where she also minored in business administration.

Summers off from school meant working at the same restaurant but when Angel's mentor and friend retired as head chef, she took over after graduation and created classic and new dishes that delighted the diners. The restaurant flourished under Angel's culinary creativity and one customer developed more than an appreciation for Angel's food. Several months after taking over the position, the young woman met her future husband at work and they have been inseparable ever since. They still live in Hyannis Port with their two children and a cocker spaniel named Buddy.

Angel Burns turned her passion for cooking and her business acumen into a thriving e-book business. She has authored several successful books on cooking different types of dishes using simple ingredients for novices and experienced chefs alike. She is still head chef in Hyannis Port and says she will probably never leave!

Author's Afterthoughts

With so many books out there to choose from, I want to thank you for choosing this one and taking precious time out of your life to buy and read my work. Readers like you are the reason I take such passion in creating these books.

It is with gratitude and humility that I express how honored I am to become a part of your life and I hope that you take the same pleasure in reading this book as I did in writing it.

Can I ask one small favour? I ask that you write an honest and open review on Amazon of what you thought of the book. This will help other readers make an informed choice on whether to buy this book.

My sincerest thanks,

Angel Burns

If you want to be the first to know about news, new books, events and giveaways, subscribe to my newsletter by

Scan QR-code

Printed in Great Britain
by Amazon